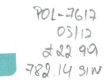
Accompaniment CDs

THE SINGERS MUSICAL THEATRE ANTHOLOGY

A collection of songs from the musical stage, categorized by voice type. The selections are presented in their authentic settings, excerpted from the original vocal scores.

ISBN-13: 978-0-634-06185-1
ISBN-10: 0-634-06185-2

HAL•LEONARD® CORPORATION

7777 W. BLUEMOUND RD. P.O. BOX 13819 MILWAUKEE, WI 53213

DISC ONE Track List

BORN TO DANCE (film)
[1] Easy to Love
(You'd Be So Easy to Love)[4]

BRIGADOON
[2] Almost Like Being in Love[2]

CABARET
[3] Tomorrow Belongs to Me[3]
[4] I Don't Care Much[1]

CHICAGO
[5] Mister Cellophane[4]

DIAMONDS
[6] What You'd Call a Dream[4]

DICK TRACY (film)
[7] What Can You Lose[4]

EASTER PARADE (film)
[8] Steppin' Out with My Baby[4]

FOLLIES
[9] Buddy's Blues[2]
[10] Make the Most of Your Music[2]

FOLLOW THE FLEET (film)
[11] I'm Putting All My Eggs
in One Basket[4]

FOOTLOOSE
[12] Mama Says[1]
[13] I Can't Stand Still[1]

THE GONDOLIERS
[14] Take a Pair of Sparkling Eyes[5]

HERCULES (film)
[15] Go the Distance[1]

**JACQUES BREL IS ALIVE AND WELL
AND LIVING IN PARIS**
[16] Amsterdam[2]

JEKYLL & HYDE
[17] Alive![3]

**JOSEPH AND THE AMAZING
TECHNICOLOR® DREAMCOAT**
[18] Any Dream Will Do[1]

Pianists on the CDs
[1] Brian Dean
[2] Ruben Piirainen
[3] Christopher Ruck
[4] Richard Walters
[5] Laura Ward

DISC TWO Track List

KISMET
- [1] Night of My Nights[2]

MARTIN GUERRE
- [2] I'm Martin Guerre[2]

THE PAJAMA GAME
- [3] Hey There[4]

PARADE
- [4] The Old Red Hills of Home[2]
- [5] This Is Not Over Yet[2]

PIPPIN
- [6] Corner of the Sky[2]

THE PIRATES OF PENZANCE
- [7] Oh, Is There Not One Maiden Breast[5]

RENT
- [8] One Song Glory[3]
- [9] Your Eyes[1]

70, GIRLS, 70
- [10] Coffee (In a Cardboard Cup)[1]

SUNSET BOULEVARD
- [11] Sunset Boulevard[2]

TITANIC
- [12] Barrett's Song[2]
- [13] The Proposal[3]
- [14] No Moon[3]

TOP HAT (film)
- [15] Isn't This a Lovely Day (To Be Caught in the Rain?)[4]

WHEN PIGS FLY
- [16] Quasimodo[4]

WORKING
- [17] The Mason[4]

Pianists on the CDs

[1] Brian Dean
[2] Ruben Piirainen
[3] Christopher Ruck
[4] Richard Walters
[5] Laura Ward

THOUGHTS ABOUT THE ACCOMPANIMENTS AND THE SONGS

We've made every effort to choose a reasonable tempo for the recorded piano accompaniments, based on cast albums or performance precedents. Other tempos could be explored for individual interpretations. We also deliberately attempted to make the accompaniment recordings musically alive, incorporating rubato, ritardandos, accelerandos, and dynamics to inspire a theatrical performance. Nevertheless, by the very nature of recording, ours is ultimately only one interpretation.

In almost all cases we recorded the accompaniments to exactly match the editions printed in *The Singer's Musical Theatre Anthology*. It is important to point out, as a reminder, that the aim of this series is a presentation of theatre literature in its original, unchanged form. Thus, we included the entire song in the printed editions. Very occasionally, when a song felt long for a stand-alone performance or audition, we eliminated a repeat in our accompaniment recording. In those instances a first ending (or D.S.) is omitted, and the accompaniment moves directly to the final ending. For your purposes, you may choose to shorten other songs for live auditions with a pianist. A few words of caution: If this is your intention, mark the score very clearly with your cuts for the audition accompanist.

Ideally, you will be using these recorded accompaniments for practice only. Because the vocal melody is not on the recording by design, you will need to learn this at the piano or another instrument. Or if you don't play well enough to plunk through the melody of a new song, and you don't have a teacher, coach or friend to help you, you may need to seek out a recording. Some words of advice, though: You will come up with a more individual interpretation, conjured from the ground up in the manner in which all the best actors work, if you learn the song on your own, built into your unique singing voice, without imitating a recorded performance.

If you are working on a duet, it is very important that you study not only your own part, but the other singer's part as well. Then you will be ready to handle any missed entrance or mistake that he or she might make in a performance, or any improvisation that comes up, and keep things on an even keel.

Choosing the right song for you and your talents is crucial in theatre music. While all actors want to stretch beyond their "type," it is important for public performances and auditions for you to know what you can do well. There are as many theories about audition literature as there are directors. But all would agree that they want to hear you at your best, not attempting something that for some reason you feel you should do, but is not your strong suit.

There are general vocal guidelines for voice types in theatre music, but these are not in stone. A soprano with a good belt may be able to sing songs from the Soprano volumes as well as the Belter volumes. Belters may work on their "head voice" in Soprano songs. Men who have voices that lie between Tenor and Baritone, commonly called "baritenors," may find songs in both the Tenor and Baritone/Bass volumes. If you have the luxury of being able to transpose music, either through your own abilities or the help of someone else, you might consider taking a song to a different key to suit your voice. Of course, the recorded accompaniments are in only the original show keys, so they won't help you in that situation.

Recording what sometimes seemed like an endless number of piano accompaniments for *The Singer's Musical Theatre Anthology* was a mammoth task. My thanks to the pianists, assistant producers and engineers who worked so graciously with me. I especially thank Brian Dean and Christopher Ruck for their committed and sustained efforts in achieving the finished results.

Surely, with hundreds of songs from a century of shows, in multiple volumes in authentic editions, any singing actor can find several songs for any occasion. Break a leg!

Richard Walters
Series Editor and Producer

ABOUT THE ENHANCED CDs

In addition to piano accompaniments playable on both your CD player and computer, these enhanced CDs also include tempo adjustment and transposition software for computer use only. This software, known as Amazing Slow Downer, was originally created for use in pop music to allow singers and players the freedom to independently adjust both tempo and pitch elements. Because we believe there may be valuable educational use for these features in classical and theatre music, we have included this software as a tool for both the teacher and student. For quick and easy installation instructions of this software, please see below.

In recording a piano accompaniment we necessarily must choose one tempo. Our choice of tempo, phrasing, *ritardandos*, and dynamics is carefully considered. But by the nature of recording, it is only one option.

However, we encourage you to explore your own interpretive ideas, which may differ from our recordings. This new software feature allows you to adjust the tempo up and down without affecting the pitch. Likewise, Amazing Slow Downer allows you to shift pitch up and down without affecting the tempo. We recommend that these new tempo and pitch adjustment features be used with care and insight. Ideally, you will be using these recorded accompaniments and Amazing Slow Downer for practice only.

The audio quality may be somewhat compromised when played through the Amazing Slow Downer. This compromise in quality will not be a factor in playing the CD audio track on a normal CD player or through another audio computer program.

INSTALLATION INSTRUCTIONS:

For Macintosh OS 8, 9 and X:
- Load the CD-ROM into your CD-ROM Drive on your computer.
- Each computer is set up a little differently. Your computer may automatically open the audio CD portion of this enhanced CD and begin to play it.
- To access the CD-ROM features, double-click on the data portion of the CD-ROM (which will have the Hal Leonard icon in red and be named as the book).
- Double-click on the "Amazing OS 8 (9 or X)" folder.
- Double-click "Amazing Slow Downer"/"Amazing X PA" to run the software from the CD-ROM, or copy this file to your hard disk and run it from there.
- Follow the instructions on-screen to get started. The Amazing Slow Downer should display tempo, pitch and mix bars. Click to select your track and adjust pitch or tempo by sliding the appropriate bar to the left or to the right.

For Windows:
- Load the CD-ROM into your CD-ROM Drive on your computer.
- Each computer is set up a little differently. Your computer may automatically open the audio CD portion of this enhanced CD and begin to play it.
- To access the CD-ROM features, click on My Computer then right click on the Drive that you placed the CD in. Click Open. You should then see a folder named "Amazing Slow Downer". Click to open the "Amazing Slow Downer" folder.
- Double-click "setup.exe" to install the software from the CD-ROM to your hard disk. Follow the on-screen instructions to complete installation.
- Go to "Start," "Programs" and find the "Amazing Slow Downer" folder. Go to that folder and select the "Amazing Slow Downer" software.
- Follow the instructions on-screen to get started. The Amazing Slow Downer should display tempo, pitch and mix bars. Click to select your track and adjust pitch or tempo by sliding the appropriate bar to the left or to the right.
- Note: On Windows NT, 2000 and XP, the user should be logged in as the "Administrator" to guarantee access to the CD-ROM drive. Please see the help file for further information.

MINIMUM SYSTEM REQUIREMENTS:

For Macintosh:
Power Macintosh; Mac OS 8.5 or higher; 4 MB Application RAM; 8x Multi-Session CD-ROM drive

For Windows:
Pentium, Celeron or equivalent processor; Windows 95, 98, ME, NT, 2000, XP; 4 MB Application RAM; 8x Multi-Session CD-ROM drive

Also Available
THE SINGER'S MUSICAL THEATRE ANTHOLOGY

Tenor, Volume 1
Book – HL00361073
Accompaniment CDs – HL00740233

ALLEGRO
You Are Never Away

ASPECTS OF LOVE
Seeing Is Believing

THE BOYS FROM SYRACUSE
Come with Me

CABARET
If You Could See Her
Sitting Pretty

CAN-CAN
I Am in Love

THE CAT AND THE FIDDLE
The Breeze Kissed Your Hair
A New Love Is Old

CATS
The Ballad of Billy M'caw

CELEBRATION
Fifty Million Years Ago

COMPANY
Being Alive
Someone Is Waiting

DO RE MI
Make Someone Happy

FANNY
Fanny

FINIAN'S RAINBOW
When I'm Not Near the Girl I Love

FLOWER DRUM SONG
You Are Beautiful

**A FUNNY THING HAPPENED ON THE
WAY TO THE FORUM**
Love, I Hear

GYPSY
All I Need Is the Girl

JESUS CHRIST SUPERSTAR
King Herod's Song

KISMET
Stranger in Paradise

LOST IN THE STARS
The Wild Justice

ME AND JULIET
The Big Black Giant
That's the Way It Happens

THE MIKADO
A Wand'ring Minstrel I

MY FAIR LADY
On the Street Where You Live

OKLAHOMA!
Kansas City

ONCE UPON A MATTRESS
Many Moons Ago

PAL JOEY
I Could Write a Book

PIPE DREAM
All Kinds of People

ROBERTA
You're Devastating

SHENANDOAH
The Only Home I Know

SOUTH PACIFIC
You've Got to Be Carefully Taught
Younger Than Springtime

STREET SCENE
Lonely House

SUNDAY IN THE PARK WITH GEORGE
Finishing the Hat

SWEENEY TODD
Johanna
Ladies and Their Sensitivities
Not While I'm Around

TWO BY TWO
I Do Not Know a Day I Did Not Love You

WISH YOU WERE HERE
Wish You Were Here

Also Available
THE SINGER'S MUSICAL THEATRE ANTHOLOGY

Tenor, Volume 2
Book – HL00747032
Accompaniment CDs – HL00740234

THE APPLE TREE
Forbidden Fruit

BEGGAR'S HOLIDAY
Maybe I Should Change My Ways

BELLS ARE RINGING
I Met a Girl

CABARET
Willkommen

CALL ME MADAM
Once Upon a Time Today

CAROUSEL
Geraniums in the Winder

CHESS
Anthem
Where I Want to Be

THE DESERT SONG
Margot

DO RE MI
I Know About Love
Asking for You

EVITA
High Flying, Adored
On This Night of a Thousand Stars

FANNY
I Like You

FIDDLER ON THE ROOF
Miracle of Miracles

FINIAN'S RAINBOW
Old Devil Moon

FLOWER DRUM SONG
Like a God

FOLLIES
Beautiful Girls

GODSPELL
All Good Gifts

GOOD NEWS
Lucky in Love

GRAND HOTEL
Love Can't Happen
At the Grand Hotel

GREASE
Alone at the Drive-In Movie

GUYS AND DOLLS
Sit Down You're Rockin' the Boat

HOW TO SUCCEED IN BUSINESS
  WITHOUT REALLY TRYING
I Believe in You

JEKYLL & HYDE
This Is the Moment

JESUS CHRIST SUPERSTAR
I Only Want to Say (Gethsemane)

JOSEPH AND THE AMAZING
  TECHNICOLOR® DREAMCOAT
Close Every Door

MILK AND HONEY
I Will Follow You

LES MISÉRABLES
Bring Him Home

MISS SAIGON
Why God Why?

THE MYSTERY OF EDWIN DROOD
Jasper's Confession

OLIVER!
Boy for Sale

ON A CLEAR DAY YOU CAN SEE FOREVER
She Wasn't You

THE PHANTOM OF THE OPERA
The Music of the Night

PLAIN AND FANCY
Young and Foolish

THE SECRET GARDEN
A Bit of Earth
Winter's on the Wing

SHE LOVES ME
Tonight at Eight
Tango Tragique
She Loves Me

THE STUDENT PRINCE
Serenade

Also Available
THE SINGER'S MUSICAL THEATRE ANTHOLOGY
Tenor, Volume 4
Book – HL00000395
Accompaniment CDs – HL00000399

AIDA
Fortune Favors the Brave

ASPECTS OF LOVE
Love Changes Everything

AVENUE Q
If You Were Gay

A CHORUS LINE
I Can Do That

A CLASS ACT
One More Beautiful Song

DO I HEAR A WALTZ?
Stay

FLOYD COLLINS
How Glory Goes

THE FULL MONTY
Breeze Off the River
Man
You Walk with Me

A FUNNY THING HAPPENED ON THE WAY TO THE FORUM
Free

GREASE
Beauty School Dropout

HAIRSPRAY
It Takes Two

INTO THE WOODS
Giants in the Sky

JEKYLL & HYDE
I Need to Know

JESUS CHRIST SUPERSTAR
Heaven on Their Minds

KISS OF THE SPIDER WOMAN
The Day After That

LADY IN THE DARK
Tschaikowsky (And Other Russians)

THE LAST FIVE YEARS
Nobody Needs to Know

THE LIGHT IN THE PIAZZA
Love to Me

THE LION KING
Endless Night

LES MISÉRABLES
What Have I Done?
Who Am I?

MOVIN' OUT
Goodnight Saigon

THE MUSIC MAN
Shipoopi

THE MYSTERY OF EDWIN DROOD
A Man Could Go Quite Mad

MYTHS AND HYMNS
Awaiting You

THE PRODUCERS
That Face
'Til Him

1776
Mama, Look Sharp

SONGS FOR NEW WORLD
King of The World

SWEET SMELL OF SUCCESS
One Track Mind

TICK, TICK ...BOOM!
Why

WICKED
Dancing Through Life

THE WILD PARTY
Let Me Drown
What Is It About Her?

YOU'RE A GOOD MAN, CHARLIE BROWN
Beethoven Day